☩Our Catholic Life
A READING AND STUDY GUIDE FOR ADULT FAITH FORMATION

5

☩ SACRAMENTS ☩

LIVING
THE
SACRAMENTS

Bill Huebsch

**TWENTY-THIRD
PUBLICATIONS**
twentythirdpublications.com

IMPRIMATUR

+ Most Reverend Joseph R. Binzer
  Auxiliary Bishop
  Archdiocese of Cincinnati
  February 9, 2016

The *Imprimatur* ("Permission to
Publish") is a declaration that a
book or pamphlet is considered
to be free of doctrinal or moral
error. It is not implied that those
who have granted the *Imprimatur*
agree with the contents, opinions,
or statements expressed.

Scripture texts are from the *New Revised Standard Version Bible:
Catholic Edition*, copyright 1989, 1993, Division of Christian Education
of the National Council of the Churches of Christ in the United States
of America. Used by permission. All rights reserved.

TWENTY-THIRD PUBLICATIONS
1 Montauk Avenue, Suite 200, New London, CT 06320
(860) 437-3012 » (800) 321-0411 » www.twentythirdpublications.com

ISBN: 978-1-62785-172-5
Library of Congress Catalog Card Number: 2016939660
Printed in the U.S.A.

Contents

How to use this study guide in seven small-group sessions

Gather. As people arrive for each session, welcome them warmly and offer them refreshments. You may wish to have sacred music playing to set the tone. If people are new to each other, name tags can help break the ice. When everyone has arrived, gather your group and invite them to open their books to today's material.

Begin with *Lectio divina* prayer. Each session opens with a short and prayerful reflection on a scriptural text that is found in that section of the *Catechism*. Here are the steps:

1. Begin with the Sign of the Cross.

2. Read aloud the Introduction for this session.

3. Call everyone to prayer using these or similar words: *Let us turn our hearts to Christ now and hear the word of the Lord.*

4. Invite a member of the group to proclaim the Scripture we present for you.

5. Invite your group members to share about the text, first in twos and threes if you wish, and then as a whole group. Sharing: *What word or phrase in this reading catches your ear? What is God saying to us in this scriptural text?*

6. Now pray in these or similar words:
   O God, we know that you are with us and that you behold all we are about to do. Now grant that, by the power of the Holy Spirit, we might be faithful as we study our faith and charitable in how we treat each other. Through Christ, our Lord. Amen.

Read. Moving around the circle in your group and rotating readers, read aloud each numbered faith statement. Group members should note items in the material that strike them as especially important. Do not read aloud the **We Believe** statements. They are provided as an enhancement to the text.

Group or personal process. When you come to the process notes, pause to continue around the circle, discussing as the notes direct. Use our suggestions as a starting point, and add your own questions, prayers, or action plans.

Finish. As you conclude this session, call everyone to prayer once again. Reread the scriptural text we used in the beginning. Then move around the circle one last time to share: *In light of this reading and what we have learned today, what has touched you most deeply? What new insight of faith will you carry away from here? What new questions about faith have arisen for you? How will today's discussion work its way into your daily life?* Close your session with the prayer we provide, or lead a spontaneous prayer in which everyone shares their own prayer.

Session One

BASED ON ARTICLES 1212–1274 OF THE *CATECHISM OF THE CATHOLIC CHURCH*. TO READ A SUMMARY OF THIS SECTION, SEE *CATECHISM* ARTICLES 1275–1284

Introduction

We kick off our study of the sacraments in the place where it all begins: baptism. We speak of it as "initiation," and it is accomplished in three sacraments together: baptism, which is the beginning of new life; confirmation, which is its strengthening; and the Eucharist, which nourishes the disciple with Christ's body and blood and leads to transformation in Christ. The essential rite of baptism consists in immersing the candidate in water, or pouring water on his or her head, while pronouncing the invocation of the Most Holy Trinity: the Father, the Son, and the Holy Spirit. Those who die for the faith, those who are catechumens, and all those who, without knowing of the Church but acting under the inspiration of grace, seek God sincerely and strive to fulfill God's will can be saved even if they have not been baptized. Since the earliest times, baptism has been administered to children because it is a grace and a gift of God that does not presuppose any human merit; children are baptized in the faith of the Church.

Scripture

READER: A reading from the Letter of Paul to the Romans.

What then are we to say? Should we continue in sin in order that grace may abound? By no means! How can we who died to sin go on living in it? Do you not know that all of us who have been baptized into Christ Jesus were baptized into his death? Therefore we have been buried with him by baptism into death, so that, just as Christ was raised from the dead by the glory of the Father, so we too might walk in newness of life. For if we have been united with him in a death like his, we will certainly be united with him in a resurrection like his. (ROMANS 6:1–5)

READER: The word of the Lord.

ALL: Thanks be to God.

PART ONE ✛ ARTICLES 1212–1228 OF THE *CATECHISM*

Initiation

[1] We Catholics celebrate three sacraments in order to become fully initiated into the People of God, the Church. The first of these is baptism, where we are born anew. The second is confirmation, which strengthens us. The third is Eucharist, which gives us the food of eternal life and continues throughout our lives.

[2] We are, in a sense, never fully initiated but always entering more deeply into the mystery of the Church and into life in Christ.

[3] In this session, we are learning about the first of these, baptism.

The term comes to us from a Greek word which means, literally, to plunge or immerse. Going into the water is a symbol of entry into Christ's death, and coming out of it a "new person" is a symbol of the resurrection.

[4] In the early Church, it was also called "the water of rebirth" or "the washing of rebirth," as we see in the Letter to Titus, chapter 3, verse 5. It has also been called "enlightenment" because by it, we enter the community in which grace and light are received and shared. Indeed, through baptism we ourselves become light for the world.

[5] The baptismal water is blessed on Holy Saturday night during the Easter Vigil. Our prayer that night reveals our understanding of baptism. We believe that grace comes to us through the sacramental signs and that this grace reveals God's unseen powers.

WE BELIEVE
Baptism is birth into new life in Christ. It is a sacrament of initiation into the community of the Church who has Christ as her head.

---

[6] We believe that water in baptism is this rich symbol. We believe that the Spirit breathes upon these waters, making them a wellspring of love. The crossing of the Red Sea by Israel in the story of the exodus from Egypt was itself a great symbol: enter into the water on one side and leave it a new people on the other.

[7] Jesus himself began his ministry by being baptized in the River Jordan and later sent his followers to baptize as well. "Go," he told them after the resurrection (in Matthew, chapter 28, verse 19). "Go...and make disciples of all nations, baptizing them in the name of the Father, and of the Son, and of the Holy Spirit..."

[8] God is love, we read in the gospels. Christ reveals that love to us in its fullness. In baptism, the Spirit enters into us because of the work of Christ: his life, death, and resurrection. In baptism, therefore, we receive the grace to love deeply, profoundly, and generously; it is the grace to move away from selfishness and sin.

[9] From the earliest days of the Church of Pentecost, baptism has been part of our practice. It has always been connected to faith: "If you believe in Jesus," Paul told his jailer in Philippi, "you will be saved." The jailer was baptized at once, with his whole family (Acts 16).

[10] St. Paul summarizes our understanding of this in his Letter to the Romans in the first verses of chapter 6 in these famous words: "Do you not know that all of us who have been baptized into Christ Jesus were baptized into his death? Therefore, we have been buried with him by baptism into death, so that, just as Christ was raised from the dead by the glory of the Father, we too might walk in newness of life."

[11] Perhaps one of the richest ways of saying this also comes from St. Paul in his Letter to the Galatians, where he says that in baptism we "put on Christ like a garment."

Group or personal process

- What does it mean for you to be baptized?

- How do you "put on Christ like a garment"?

- How does being baptized into the death of Christ, as we learned in faith statement #10, lead you to practice the art of self-giving love?

How we celebrate

[12] From the earliest years of the Church, the journey to become Christian has occurred in certain clear stages. A person hears the word proclaimed, accepts the gospel, turns his or her heart to Christ, professes his or her faith, is baptized, receives the Holy Spirit, and begins receiving the Eucharist.

[13] Some of these moments are observed with rites within the catechumenate. Where infant baptism is the norm, this process is greatly abridged but it is assumed there will be catechesis and conversion at a later time. Where adult baptism is being done, the Church provides for a process known as the Rite of Christian Initiation of Adults, called, in short, the RCIA.

[14] In the Eastern traditions, infants receive baptism but also immediately confirmation and Eucharist; in the Latin tradition, the baptism of infants is followed by years of catechesis before the sacraments of confirmation and Eucharist are received.

What it all means

[15] When we look at the rite of baptism, the meaning of the sacrament emerges clearly. We begin with the sign of the cross, which traces on the body the imprint of Christ in the paschal mystery. Next we proclaim the word of God, because the light of faith flows from that, and baptism is inseparable from faith. We then signify our liberation from selfishness and sin by publicly rejecting evil and sin at its source and by anointing the person with oil.

[16] It is in the baptismal promises that we reject the works of darkness and sin, and it is excellent to renew them often. After we make these promises, we confess our faith with the Creed and prepare for the rite of immersion. The baptismal water is then blessed by calling down the Spirit so that those baptized may live in that Spirit.

[17] Next comes the essential element of the sacrament. This is the actual moment of baptism. The person being baptized is three times immersed in water, or water is symbolically poured three times on the head. This signifies entry into the death of Christ and thereby entry into the new life of Christ, and that is the same as entry into the Church.

[18] Having holy water in our homes and using it to remind ourselves of our baptism is an excellent way to live our faith every day!

WE BELIEVE

The essential rite of baptism consists in immersing the candidate in water or pouring water on his or her head while invoking the Holy Trinity: Father, Son, and Spirit.

---

[19] In the Latin tradition, the minister prays as the person is immersed: "[Name], I baptize you in the name of the Father, and of the Son, and of the Holy Spirit." In the Eastern traditions, the person being baptized turns east and the minister says: "The servant of God, [Name], is baptized in the name of the Father, and of the Son, and of the Holy Spirit."

[20] In the Latin tradition, we next anoint the newly baptized with sacred chrism, which is a lovely perfumed oil consecrated by the bishop; this holy oil signifies the gift of the Spirit. In the Eastern

traditions, we next confirm the baptized in the sacrament of confirmation. Then we cover the person in a white garment symbolizing the putting on of Christ, and finally we light a candle for them, taking the flame from the Easter candle. This symbolizes the light of Christ which is in their hearts now as newly baptized persons.

[21] The newly baptized is now celebrated as a child of God and is entitled to pray aloud the "Our Father." In the Eastern traditions, the newly baptized immediately receives Eucharist, which completes the initiation. In the Latin tradition, newly baptized infants wait several years to receive Eucharist, but adults may receive Eucharist at the same liturgy. We then conclude the rite with a solemn blessing.

Group or personal process

- When you review the rite of baptism, what touches you most?

- What part gives you a deep sense of the beauty and power of this rite?

- Why is it important for parishes to celebrate this sacrament in the midst of the whole assembly during Mass on Sundays?

PART THREE + ARTICLES 1246–1274 OF THE CATECHISM

Who can be baptized?

[22] Before they are baptized, people should be prepared. The normal way to do that is in the catechumenate, an ancient practice of the Church that was restored at Vatican II.

[23] The first step for those preparing for baptism, of course, is the turning of their hearts to Christ. One might encounter Christ in the Church, of course, but also in one's family and friends; one might see Christ in people who live the gospel well or in liturgy, prayer, or charity; likewise, one might encounter Christ through formation and education materials used in RCIA or formation programs.

[24] But we also baptize infants who are clearly too young to experience any of this firsthand. Children are born into a world where darkness sometimes seems to surround us. Baptism initiates them into a community where grace is shared. And only grace helps us to be light in that darkness.

[25] Baptism is the first step on the journey of faith that will last a lifetime. Infants have been baptized since the early years of Church life, and we continue that practice today. "Baptism is the sacrament of faith," the *Catechism* tells us in article 1253. "But faith needs the community of believers. It is only within the faith of the Church that each of the faithful can believe."

[26] The faith required for baptism is not a perfect and mature faith but a new faith that will grow and mature with the person. The whole community is called to support and nurture faith, but this is especially true for parents and family members or baptismal sponsors.

[27] Normally, bishops and priests preside at baptism, in addition to deacons in the Latin tradition. However, anyone can baptize, even someone who is not himself or herself already baptized, if it is necessary and if the intention is correct.

The necessity of baptism

[28] For those to whom the gospel is proclaimed and who are able to ask for the sacrament, baptism is necessary for salvation. But while we believe God has made baptism necessary, we also believe that God is not bound by the sacraments, and we trust the mercy of God.

[29] We believe that those who die for their faith without being baptized live and die in God's mercy. We believe that catechumens who die before baptism are also in God's mercy and love.

WE BELIEVE

The grace of baptism includes forgiveness from sin, new life in the Church, being an adopted son or daughter of God, and the power of the Holy Spirit.

---

[30] Furthermore, we believe that all those who are not aware of the gospel but who seek truth and follow God's will based on how they understand that also live in God's mercy and love. And finally, children who die without baptism are fully entrusted to the mercy of God, and we do not believe God is absent from them.

Grace

[31] In baptism, we believe, all occasions of sin and of being selfish and unilateral are forgiven. And yet the inclination to such sin remains—as does suffering, death, and weakness of character. It is up to us, as the Letter of Timothy suggests, to till the soil of our souls well.

[32] In baptism we become adopted sons and daughters of God. We receive sanctifying grace, which empowers us to live our faith.

Baptism makes us members of the body of Christ, which makes us "members of one another" and incorporates us into the Church.

[33] Baptism gives us a share in the common priesthood of all believers. We are called thereby to serve each other, to listen to Church leaders and obey them, to assemble for the Eucharist, and to be nourished with the word of God.

[34] And while this is true for us Catholics, we also recognize the baptisms of all other Christians and we call them sisters and brothers. Indeed, baptism is the sacramental bond of all Christians. Baptism connects us to Christ and seals us with an indelible mark that identifies us as "Christian."

[35] For this reason, baptism cannot be repeated. The seal of baptism commits us to the life of grace we just described above. And those who live by this seal—remembering it always, and dying "marked with the sign of faith—will know God, Christ, and the Holy Spirit. God will love them eternally.

Group or personal process

• In your own words, what are your baptismal promises?

• Why is it important for us to be actively engaged in a parish? What do you give to your parish? What does your parish give to you?

• As a member of the common priesthood, what roles and responsibilities do you have toward the Church and the world around you?

Prayer

Jesus, source of grace and teacher of us all, may our baptism lead us to become faithful disciples of you. May we continually reject darkness and sin in order to embrace the light of your truth. We pray now that the Spirit you sent may turn our hearts toward you so that we might walk with you in our daily lives and learn how to build the reign of God here on earth. We pray in your holy name. Amen.

Session Two

CONFIRMATION

BASED ON ARTICLES 1285–1314 OF THE *CATECHISM OF THE CATHOLIC CHURCH*. TO READ A SUMMARY OF THIS SECTION, SEE *CATECHISM* ARTICLES 1315–1321

Introduction

Confirmation is very closely connected to baptism because it perfects baptismal grace; it is the sacrament that confers the Holy Spirit in order to incorporate us more firmly into Christ, strengthen our bond with the Church, and help us bear witness to the Christian faith. In the Eastern rites, confirmation is administered immediately after baptism and is followed by participation in the Eucharist; this tradition highlights the unity of the three sacraments of Christian initiation. In the West, a candidate for confirmation who has attained the age of reason must profess the faith, be in the state of grace, have the intention of receiving the sacrament, and be prepared to assume the role of disciple and witness to Christ, both within the ecclesial community and in temporal affairs. The essential rite of confirmation is anointing the forehead of the baptized with sacred chrism (in the East other sense organs as well), together with the laying on of the minister's hand and the words "Be sealed with the gift of the Holy Spirit."

Scripture

READER: A reading from the Acts of the Apostles.

When the day of Pentecost had come, they were all together in one place. And suddenly from heaven there came a sound like the rush of a violent wind, and it filled the entire house where they were sitting. Divided tongues, as of fire, appeared among them, and a tongue rested on each of them. All of them were filled with the Holy Spirit and began to speak in other languages, as the Spirit gave them ability. (ACTS OF THE APOSTLES 2:1–4)

READER: The word of the Lord.

ALL: Thanks be to God.

PART ONE **✦ ARTICLES 1285–1292 OF THE** *CATECHISM*

The spirit of the Lord

[1] Let us begin by saying clearly here that confirmation is intimately connected to both baptism and Eucharist. They are all sacraments of initiation, adding to and completing each other. The reception of all three sacraments is required in order for initiation to be complete.

[2] We must also begin by saying once again that God revealed his love to us completely and fully in Christ. At Jesus' own baptism the Spirit descended on him, fulfilling what Isaiah had said in chapter 11, verse 2: "The spirit of the Lord shall rest on him, the spirit of wisdom and understanding, the spirit of counsel and might, the spirit of knowledge and awe in the face of God."

[3] This is the Holy Spirit of God. Jesus was conceived in this Spirit; his entire mission was rooted in love and was in complete communion with God his Father, one God, forever and ever.

[4] When you read Acts of the Apostles, it is clear that this Spirit deeply touched the apostles. It filled their hearts with the fire of love and gave them courage, hope, and strength. And most strikingly, through this same Spirit, Peter and the others found the words to communicate the wonders of God through preaching; the Spirit touched other hearts so still more were added to their number.

[5] And on and on and on...down through the centuries right up to this present moment: wherever you are, the Spirit is with you. From the earliest years of the Church, the apostles laid hands on the newly baptized, conferring on them the gift of the Spirit and completing the grace of baptism.

WE BELIEVE

Confirmation perfects baptismal grace. Through this sacrament, the Holy Spirit takes root in us, and we are incorporated ever more deeply into the body of Christ. Our bond with Christ and the Church and our commitment to her mission are increased.

[6] But also very early in our history was added an anointing with holy oil, also called "chrism." This was added to the laying on of hands. In fact, the name "Christian" means, literally, "one who is anointed." The anointing signifies the gift of the Spirit who brings comfort, courage, and counsel to us.

[7] Ever since those early years, this ceremony of anointing has continued in both the Eastern traditions and the Latin tradition. The

Eastern traditions do not refer to this sacrament as confirmation but rather as "chrismation." The Latin tradition calls it confirmation, which suggests that baptism is confirmed or ratified and that baptismal grace is thereby strengthened.

Two traditions: east and west

[8] In the early years of the Church baptism and confirmation were celebrated as one sacrament. Most of the time it was celebrated one time each year at the Easter Vigil. But soon infant baptisms became more common and were celebrated throughout the year. Soon more and more rural parishes were added and dioceses grew in size. Bishops were no longer present for every baptism as had been the custom.

[9] All of this led (in the Latin tradition) to the separation of baptism and confirmation. In the Eastern traditions they remain united, with the priest presiding at confirmation as well as at baptism, using oils blessed by the bishop.

[10] Beyond all this, a "double anointing" became the custom in the Church at Rome, and this also facilitated the separation of the two sacraments. The first anointing was done by the priest as the newly baptized came out of the water. The second was done by the bishop.

[11] So today, in our rite of baptism the priest still performs that first anointing which signifies the entrance of the newly baptized into the priestly, prophetic, and royal roles of Christ in the Church. But when an adult is being baptized, there is only one anointing, and it is in the sacrament of confirmation with the baptizing priest presiding.

[12] The Eastern practice of uniting the two anointings emphasizes the unity of Christian initiation. The Latin practice of dividing

them when confirming children and youth emphasizes the connection with the bishop as the chief pastor of each parish.

Group or personal process

- How do you experience the work of the Holy Spirit in your life?

- For what aspect of your life, your work, or your ministry do you need courage, strength, and wisdom?

PART TWO ✦ ARTICLES 1293–1305 OF THE *CATECHISM*

Sacred oil

[13] We use oil to anoint. Anointing with oil is ancient and rich in meaning. Oil is a sign of abundance and joy according to the beautiful words of Psalm 23: "You prepare a table before me...you anoint my head with oil; my cup overflows!"

[14] Oil cleanses, and we bathe with it. It limbers, and we use it to soothe our muscles. It is a sign of healing, and we use it to soothe our bruises and wounds. It makes radiant with beauty, health, and strength.

[15] In the sacramental life of the Church, oil carries all these meanings. We anoint catechumens to strengthen them and give them wisdom. We anoint the sick to express healing and comfort. We anoint in baptism as a sign of the Holy Spirit who leads us to holiness. Likewise, anointing in confirmation gives the one confirmed a more complete share in the mission of Christ and the Church.

[16] Those confirmed are marked in this sacrament, as at baptism, with the seal of the Holy Spirit and the sign of faith. Remember that in the sacraments it is Christ who acts on our behalf. In confirmation Christ puts his seal upon our hearts in order to claim us, as it were, and to make us his own. And we, for our part, gladly receive the Spirit.

How we celebrate

[17] The blessing of this sacred oil, then, is really the first action of this sacrament even though it occurs at another time and in another liturgy. Bishops consecrate or bless these oils at the chrism Mass that takes place in every diocese each year prior to the Triduum.

WE BELIEVE

Confirmation marks our souls permanently; therefore we can only be confirmed one time.

---

[18] In the Latin tradition or when confirmation is separated from baptism, the liturgy of confirmation begins with the renewal of baptismal promises and a profession of faith. When adults are baptized, they immediately receive confirmation and Eucharist. This usually occurs at the Easter Vigil, and the presider is usually a priest. But for young people, Eucharist often precedes confirmation, and the celebration of confirmation normally occurs at a time of year that is convenient to both the local parish and the bishop.

[19] In some dioceses, because of the great numbers, bishops may designate a local pastor to preside. When the bishop is present he extends his hands over the whole group of those to be confirmed, and he prays for the Holy Spirit to be upon them.

[20] The essential rite of the sacrament follows. The bishop anoints each on the forehead with chrism, saying as he does: "Be sealed with the gift of the Holy Spirit." In the Eastern traditions, several parts of the body are anointed: forehead, eyes, nose and ears, lips, breast, back, hands, and feet. The rite concludes with the sign of peace, which signifies the union of the bishop with all the faithful.

The gifts of confirmation

[21] God is love, the Scriptures tell us, and this love is revealed to us fully in Christ, the Son of God. The Spirit is poured fully into our hearts, awakening in us the seeds of eternity and continuing the miracle of Pentecost in our own day and age. Hence, we can say that confirmation roots us more deeply in love, unites us more closely to Christ, increases in us the gifts of the Spirit, and binds us more tightly to the Church.

[22] Because of confirmation, we receive a special strength to live our faith more fully, to witness to what we believe, and never to be ashamed of dying and rising in Jesus Christ. Like baptism, confirmation is received only once because it marks us permanently in faith.

Group or personal process

- To whom do you think it is most necessary for Christians to witness to their faith? Legend tells us that St. Francis of Assisi once suggested that Christians should always witness to their faith—and when necessary, to use words to do so! How do you do that?

- Make a list of the attitudes, expectations, or opportunities in your own culture that challenge your faith? How does your baptism and confirmation help you maintain your Christian values?

Who is confirmed?

[23] Everyone who is baptized but not yet confirmed should receive this sacrament. Without it, baptism is still valid and we are members of the Church, but initiation is incomplete. In the Latin tradition, young adulthood is the normal age to receive this sacrament, but children in danger of death may also be confirmed.

[24] This sacrament is not meant to mark entry into "adult faith." Spiritual maturity is not linked to chronological age. Indeed, living the mystery of our faith—dying in Christ, rising to new life, and living daily life in the Spirit—begins at baptism. Many young people achieve this maturity.

[25] In the Latin tradition, where confirmation and baptism are separated by several years, preparation for confirmation is important. It should focus on the ever deeper "conversion" or the turning of our hearts to Christ. It should prepare the Christian to work in the mission of the Church and awaken a sense of *belonging*.

WE BELIEVE

To be confirmed in the Latin rite, a candidate must be old enough to understand, profess his or her faith, be in the state of grace, choose confirmation freely, and be ready to take on the role of a disciple.

[26] In the final period of preparation, those to be confirmed should undergo a retreat and cleansing of the heart. They should be aware that God is communicating God's own self to them and revealing to them the divine heart. In a word, they should be aware that they

are "living in grace." Preparation might include sacramental reconciliation, intense prayer, and personal reflection.

[27] Finally, those preparing for confirmation should seek the help of a companion or sponsor—if possible, a baptismal godparent. In the end, for those in the Latin tradition, preparation should result in persons who are ready to receive this sacrament freely once they are old enough. They should be living in grace, desire the sacrament, and be ready to assume the role of disciple.

Who presides?
[28] In the Eastern traditions, the priest presides at this sacrament using sacred chrism blessed by the bishop; this expresses the unity of the Church. In the Latin tradition, the same is true when confirmation is received by adults who are being baptized and confirmed in the same rite or who are being received into full communion from another Christian Church that does not have valid confirmation.

[29] In danger of death, of course, priests may confirm at any time. In all other settings, the bishop presides at confirmation unless, as we said above, he designates a local pastor to preside.

Changes
[30] Confirmation is a sacrament that is under study within the Catholic community. In some dioceses of the Latin tradition in the United States, a new order of receiving baptism, confirmation, and Eucharist has been established. In these dioceses confirmation is received before first Eucharist, "restoring the order" of the early Church.

[31] The decision to do this is based on our theology, which tells us that *Eucharist completes initiation*. In most dioceses, on the oth-

er hand, students are confirmed at age twelve or fourteen or older. The key is this: regardless the age or order received, *we must live in Christ*. We must turn our hearts to God and "put on Christ like a garment" over and over again throughout our lives under the power of the Spirit.

Group or personal process

- How has the sacrament of confirmation helped you to face the challenges of being a Catholic Christian in today's world?

- What role does the Holy Spirit play in guiding your choices?

- In your own words, what does it mean to be a disciple?

Prayer

Come, Holy Spirit. Come. Fill our hearts with the fire of your love. Fill our Church with your mercy and forgiveness. Fill our world with the love of Christ. Come, Holy Spirit. Come. Make us into temples of your wisdom and strength. Be with us as we live our faith. We pray through Christ, our Lord. Amen.

Session Three

EUCHARIST

BASED ON ARTICLES 1322–1405 OF THE *CATECHISM OF THE CATHOLIC CHURCH*. TO READ A SUMMARY OF THIS SECTION, SEE *CATECHISM* ARTICLES 1406–1419

Introduction

We turn now to consider how baptism and confirmation lead to Eucharist. The Eucharist is the heart and the summit of the Church's life. The Eucharistic celebration always includes the proclamation of the word of God; thanksgiving to God the Father for all his benefits, above all the gift of his Son; the consecration of bread and wine; and participation in the liturgical banquet by receiving the Lord's body and blood. Christ himself, acting through the ministry of the priest, offers the Eucharistic sacrifice. The essential signs of the Eucharistic sacrament are wheat bread and grape wine on which the blessing of the Holy Spirit is invoked and the priest pronounces the words of consecration spoken by Jesus during the Last Supper: "This is my body which will be given up for you...This is the cup of my blood..."

Scripture

READER: A reading from the Gospel of John.

After he had washed their feet, had put on his robe, and had returned to the table, he said to them, "Do you know what I have done to you? You call me Teacher and Lord—and you are right, for that is what I am. So if I, your Lord and Teacher, have washed your feet, you also ought to wash one another's feet. For I have set you an example, that you also should do as I have done to you." (JOHN 13:12–15)

READER: The word of the Lord.

ALL: Thanks be to God.

PART ONE ✛ ARTICLES 1322–1344 OF THE *CATECHISM*

Source and summit

[1] Each time we celebrate the Eucharist, we deepen and more perfectly complete our own Christian initiation. We enter ever more deeply into Christ, putting on Christ more fully as a garment and living with Christ forever. The great *Dogmatic Constitution on the Church* from Vatican II makes this clear in a single, memorable line: The Eucharist, it explains simply, is "the source and summit of the Christian life."

[2] All the rest of the work of the Church, and indeed, the daily life of us Christians, directs us toward the Eucharist and flows from it. It is the source of our union together as the People of God. It is, you might say, an entire summary of our faith wrapped up in a single moment where Christ acts to express the love that he revealed in his life and death and that is now sustained by the Spirit.

Many names

[3] Because it is so central to us and so rich, we give this sacrament many names. Each name reflects certain dimensions of this diamond, and in each we see a slightly different meaning. The word

"Eucharist" itself comes from Greek and means, literally, "thanks-giving."

[4] We also refer to it as "The Lord's Supper" because it flows from that famous last supper which Jesus shared with his friends. We call it "The Breaking of Bread" because in that last supper Jesus used the rite of breaking and sharing bread, a rite that was common for Jews. It was again in that rite where his disciples recognized him after the resurrection, and it was that rite around which his early followers gathered, using it to signify their own unity as the body of Christ.

[5] We call it "The Eucharistic assembly" because the Eucharist is celebrated in public by the Church assembled. We refer to the Eucharist as "the memorial of the Lord's passion and resurrection," "the holy sacrifice," and "sacrifice of praise." We call it "holy com-munion." We call it "the Mass," by which we refer to its final action which sends us forth to love and serve and which was rendered, in Latin, *ita missa est.*

Important signs

[6] Each and every time we gather faithfully to celebrate the Eucharist, Christ makes himself present among us under the signs of bread and wine. This is the memorial he left us: to share this meal and in it to recognize his presence in our midst. This reflects our Jewish roots because, at least from the time of Abraham, bread and wine were offered in sacrifice to show gratitude to God. Also, it was unleavened bread that they ate on that night of the Passover, marking their imminent departure on a journey during which they were fed with manna.

[7] The cup of blessing at the end of the Jewish Passover meal was a hopeful and festive action and a sign of God among them. In Christ,

this blessing cup became a sharing in the kingdom of God. In Christ, this bread became a sharing in his dying and rising.

[8] Perhaps the most revealing moment in Jesus' life came on the night of that famous supper when he revealed the depths of his love. As a servant would do, he rose from the supper table, donned an apron, and washed the feet of his disciples. In this single act, he forcefully revealed that God is love.

WE BELIEVE

The Eucharist is the source of the Church's life and the summit of it as well. Everything we do flows from the Eucharist, and our entire life is oriented to being the body of Christ.

---

[9] Matthew, Mark, and Luke hand on to us the account of the breaking of bread, while John adds the account of the washing of feet. By reading them in their entirety, we get the picture clearly: Christ has left us a memorial of his love, a way to continue to make himself present down through the centuries.

[10] In turn we are challenged to live our life as one of service and communion. He told us to do likewise. Here for us is a "new Passover," one in which Jesus passes over to his Father and one in which we too pass over to new life, which is why it is always initiation.

[11] This liturgical action is more than a mere memory, however, for in it Christ continues to be present, forming us in love, shaping us as a people, and loving us to death. From the very beginning, the followers of Christ have gathered for this memorial. We gather too using the same fundamental prayer, around the entire world, on the first day of the week. *It is the center of our lives.*

Group or personal process

- What does it mean to you that Jesus served his followers by "washing their feet" as he did?

- How does the Eucharist challenge you?

- How does participating in Mass and receiving communion week after week set a cadence or pace for your spiritual journey?

PART TWO + ARTICLES 1345–1374 OF THE *CATECHISM*

How we celebrate

[12] The way we celebrate the Eucharist today reflects closely how it was celebrated in the early Church communities. The liturgy has a certain defined structure following two great parts: Liturgy of the Word and Liturgy of the Eucharist. Together they form one single act of worship.

[13] Remember the story of Emmaus? The liturgy follows that basic format: Jesus walks with us to teach us and then sits with us at table. First, we gather faithfully together, coming from all walks of life, from all cultures, and from many places, into a single place with one mind, sharing one heart and one faith. Christ presides, represented by the priest, but all who gather participate fully.

[14] We read from the Scriptures, both the Old and New Testaments. We hear a homily and we pray faithfully. We present the bread and wine along with other offerings that symbolize our daily lives, our re-

sources, and our gifts—and these are blessed by the Spirit. And then the moment arrives for us to pray the great Eucharistic Prayer of the Church, giving thanks, committing ourselves, and being made holy.

[15] It begins with a preface expressing this thanks, after which we sing with full heart and soul. In the prayer over the gifts we acknowledge that it is the Spirit who blesses us and our gifts to make them and us into the body of Christ. By retelling the story of the Lord's Supper in the power of this Holy Spirit, Christ's body and blood are made sacramentally present under the form of bread and wine.

WE BELIEVE

The Mass always includes the proclamation of the word, thanksgiving to God, the consecration of bread and wine, and participation in Holy Communion. These all combine into one single act of worship.

---

[16] By remembering the story of God loving us and the dying and rising of Christ, our own hearts fill with gratitude. By calling to mind then the entire Church—living and dead, our pastors and leaders and all the faithful—we connect ourselves in the Spirit. And then in communion we all share in this great sacramental moment when Christ fills us with love.

Thanksgiving and praise

[17] In the Eucharist we pray in two important ways. First, we give thanks to God for the great love shown to us through Christ. Second, we celebrate and sing praise to God, who is the generous giver of all these gifts. The Eucharist is also the memorial of Christ's love, and every time we remember this love, it becomes more real for us and more present in our own lives.

[18] Tremendous grace flows from the Eucharist because in it we see into the heart of God as clearly as humanly possible. All the many ways in which we sin, the ways we live selfishly, and the ways we break our bond with the community are focused here.

[19] We are forgiven again, and again, and again. The Eucharist is, in this way, a sacrifice: "an action that makes us holy." It is Christ's action, the power of grace, the forgiveness of sins, and the celebration of Holy Communion. We bring our whole lives to this, our work and suffering and love, our failures to love and our desires, our fear and anger and ignorance, our joy and hope and communion.

[20] So it is the whole Church who prays at Eucharist, in every time and place where it is celebrated. This includes the entire communion of saints. When we gather faithfully, Christ is present, the power of the Spirit heals us, and God is once again expressed fully.

Group or personal process

• What is your own experience of gathering for Eucharist?

• What happens within you during these celebrations?

• How does Eucharist touch your life?

• How do you take your experience of the Mass home with you?

Real presence

[21] Christ is present in the Church in many ways. We find him among the poor and rejected, whom he loves; we find him in the word broken open and shared; he is likewise found in the gathering of the people, in all of the sacraments, and in the person of the priest or bishop as they exercise the ministry of the Church. But Christ is present especially in the Eucharist.

[22] When we speak of "real" presence in Eucharist, we do not mean to exclude the other types of presence that we have just mentioned. We mean only to emphasize that here in the Eucharist, Christ is present in a substantial way, a unique way, fully, really, and entirely. Christ makes himself present to us in the Eucharist.

[23] Christ makes himself present in the bread and wine in this sacrament. The priest pronounces the words of Christ from the Lord's Supper, but the power to transform the bread is God's. We give a name to this daily miracle, a name that helps us see that the presence of which we speak is a substantial one. The name is "transubstantiation," and by it we refer to the belief that the very substance of the bread and wine actually changes.

[24] It is for this reason that we bow or genuflect when we pass the tabernacle. It is for this reason that we revere the Eucharist and for this reason that we set aside some Eucharistic hosts for the sick and for our own adoration. It is for this reason that we place our tabernacle in a worthy and safe location.

[25] Christ himself gave this memorial of his love to his closest friends and disciples, and now he remains mysteriously present in

our midst, still loving us, still giving us grace, and still present. Do not try to understand this with your senses, as St. Thomas Aquinas reminds us, but give yourself over to this miracle. Gather with others who believe; break open and share the word; then turn to the gifts of bread and wine with an ordained priest, who represents Christ.

WE BELIEVE

Holy Communion increases our union with the Lord, forgives venial sins, and helps us live in grace. It reinforces the body of Christ.

---

[26] Invoke the Holy Spirit and retell the great story of that great, loving supper; give thanks for all we have received; and lo! Christ makes himself present! We then receive Communion, as the Church urges us to do each time we are present at Mass. It is Christ whom we receive.

[27] Just as in baptism we enter into the death of the Lord so as to die to ourselves and rise with Christ, so in Eucharist we once again share in the cross. For this reason, receiving communion is something we do only after preparation. We should first examine our consciences and be free of the kind of serious sin that separates us from the community; we call these "mortal sins."

[28] If such serious sin has occurred, sacramental reconciliation should precede our celebration of the Eucharist. We should fast from other food for one hour beforehand and receive this gift with humility and joy. The Church requires that we celebrate the Eucharist each Sunday and on all holy days of obligation, and it obliges us to receive communion at least once a year during the Easter Season.

[29] It's important to note that, even though Christ is fully present when we receive only the bread, the sign of communion is more complete when given under both bread and wine. This is the usual form of receiving communion in the Eastern rites.

Communion with Christ

[30] The key to the Eucharist is this: *we become what we receive*. When we celebrate the Eucharist, we Christians join more closely to Christ and to one another. Indeed, we become the body of Christ! In this process we are freed to live in Christ and to live with love and to shed our sinful behavior.

WE BELIEVE

Christ himself is present in this sacrament through the word, the community, the ministry of the Church, and especially in the bread and wine.

---

[31] For how can we be joined to one another and not love? In this way, by repeating the Eucharist over and over and over again, our journey of faith is empowered. Just as the drum beat provides the cadence of a song, regular Eucharist provides a steady rhythm to our shared life in the Church.

[32] Hence we are joined to one another and to the poor, the rejected, and the outcast; we are joined to Christ. And finally, the Eucharist and our gathering for it—the great singing and praying of the Church—also expresses the hope we have that one day we will live in this love forever. One day, we will have the joy of knowing God revealed to us in Christ, and we will live in the Spirit.

Group or personal process

- How do you experience yourself being the body of Christ? How does this affect your daily life?

- Working together as a small group, compile a list of all those who are part of the body of Christ but whom you perceive feel "left out." What can you personally and your parish/community of faith do to make them feel more welcome?

- Read faith statement #32 again and talk about how the Eucharist calls us to works of mercy on behalf of Christ.

Prayer

Jesus, you give us yourself in the Eucharist and invite us to become your body. May we be worthy of this great calling and always embrace it with love and commitment. We now turn our hearts once again to you as we recall your selfless love for us. We listen for your voice as it sounds in our hearts in these quiet moments. Our hearts fill with awe and gratitude as we contemplate your mercy toward us. Make us, we pray, merciful likewise toward one another. We pray in your holy name. Amen.

Session Four

BASED ON ARTICLES 1420–1484 OF THE *CATECHISM OF THE CATHOLIC CHURCH*. TO READ A SUMMARY OF THIS SECTION, SEE *CATECHISM* ARTICLES 1485–1498

Introduction

Having considered the three sacraments of initiation, let us turn our attention now to two sacraments of healing and forgiveness. The forgiveness of sins committed after baptism is conferred by a particular sacrament called the sacrament of conversion, confession, penance, or reconciliation. The movement of return to God, called conversion and repentance, entails sorrow for and abhorrence of sins committed and the firm purpose of sinning no more in the future. The essential rite of the sacrament of reconciliation consists of the penitent's repentance, confession of sins to the priest, the intention to make reparation, and the priest's words of absolution and blessing. The spiritual effects of the sacrament of reconciliation are reconciliation with God by which the penitent recovers grace; reconciliation with the Church; peace and serenity of conscience, and spiritual consolation; and an increase of spiritual strength.

Scripture

READER: A reading from the Second Letter of Paul to the Corinthians.

So if anyone is in Christ, there is a new creation: everything old has passed away; see, everything has become new! All this is from God, who reconciled us to himself through Christ, and has given us the ministry of reconciliation; that is, in Christ God was reconciling the world to himself, not counting their trespasses against them, and entrusting the message of reconciliation to us. (2 Corinthians 5:17–19)

READER: The word of the Lord.

ALL: Thanks be to God.

PART ONE + ARTICLES 1420–1437 OF THE *CATECHISM*
Forgiveness

[1] God forgives us endlessly, and the Church celebrates this reality through the sacrament of reconciliation. For even though we are baptized and confirmed, and even though we are steeped in Eucharist, there remains that tendency within us to sin, to be selfish, and to fail to love.

[2] But God never fails to love and the Church celebrates this in the sacrament of reconciliation. We call it a sacrament of "conversion" because in celebrating it we turn our hearts back to love through Christ. The term "penance" comes from a Latin word *repere,* which suggests a posture of sorrow and a process of change.

[3] It is also called "confession" because it is in this experience that we are invited to speak aloud about how we sin, and in that speaking aloud, we recognize the mercy of God. And it is called the sacrament of "reconciliation" because it draws us back to balance and reconnects us to our journey of faith as it celebrates God's wonderful love.

Mark's gospel

[4] If one of the gospels serves as a reflection on this, it is the Gospel of Mark. Time and again in this gospel the writer reminds us that, if we wish to follow Christ, we must "repent." Indeed, the first words the writer puts on the lips of Jesus are a call to turn our hearts to God, to see how it is that we do indeed fail to love, to repent from that, and to believe in the Good News.

WE BELIEVE

The forgiveness of sins after baptism is experienced through a sacrament called the sacrament of conversion, confession, penance, or reconciliation.

---

[5] All of this is wrapped up in a new understanding that Jesus made the center of his teaching, namely, that the reign of God is *at hand*! This gospel, written in the earliest communities of Christians, is a call to enter into this new way of living with a profound commitment. It is a call to be baptized with the baptism with which Jesus was baptized: to die and to rise in Christ.

[6] When we die to ourselves in loving others and continually correct our course in life to keep us on that journey of faith, we encounter God. This course correction is the purpose of this sacrament. It's a time to allow the Spirit to enter us and draw us back to love.

Our inner lives

[7] This isn't about public displays of sorrow but about the condition of our own hearts. It is a deep turning or reorientation of our lives which is then given a visible sign. It is a deep desire to change our lives and, indeed, a sort of inner and sometimes painful recog-

nition that we have hurt ourselves and others by the things we have done or the things we have failed to do.

[8] When we pause to admit to our sins, our hearts are heavy and burdened, but God gives us a "new heart." We start all over again, refreshed by God's love, and ready to take on the world!

Saying we're sorry

[9] There are many ways to correct our course and light our interior lamps of love: fasting, prayer, almsgiving, reconciling with others, caring for those in need, and dying to ourselves in loving others. We can also work for justice and peace, fight for what is right in our society, develop a heart for the materially poor, or set a course for our lives that results in us being conscious about how we live and love.

[10] As important as all of the above practices and disciplines are for our lives, we must always root ourselves in the practice of worship and prayer, especially celebrating Eucharist and prayerfully reading the Scriptures.

Group or personal process

- Of the ways mentioned above, which do you find most helpful in "correcting the course" of your life?

- Prepare for yourself a short list of things you can do to better correct your course on your journey of faith. Add to this list one or two new ways of reconciliation, such as fasting, prayer, or almsgiving.

- Share about your experience with this sacrament? How has it led you to greater life in Christ?

Only God forgives

[11] The Greek word in the gospels that is often translated as "sin" is better translated as "missing the mark." An archer with a bent arrow cannot hit the target. The arrow will fly off in an errant direction and the archer will have to chase after it, straighten it out, and then try again. We are like that arrow: we are made for love alone, and when we fail to love well, we miss our mark.

[12] In this sense we fail our created purpose, but we also fail our companions. In the sacrament of reconciliation we celebrate a reality that is always there but that we sometimes forget: that God forgives us. The Church is an instrument of this forgiveness and seeks to draw us back to God.

[13] Indeed, we are a sign to the world that God will never, ever cease loving. No matter how deep the darkness, the light of love still shines!

[14] There is also a certain public dimension to this. Even though how we miss the mark seems terribly private to us, each time we do that, we also hurt others. So in reconciliation we are reunited with each other and can sit down together at supper again. Christ repeatedly invited those whom he had forgiven to dine with him, and this shocked some religious authorities.

[15] We all miss the mark sometimes, so this sacrament is meant for everyone. The Church has only one task: to express the love of God and to help us see that we are set free to live as we were created and to love as we are empowered. In the first step of reconciliation, the Spirit leads us to turn our hearts to see how we sin, name that

clearly, and take actions to change. Sometimes this involves personal sin and other times social sin.

WE BELIEVE

The sacrament of reconciliation has three actions on the part of the penitent: repentance, confession, and the intention to make reparation.

[16] In the second step, the Church announces to us that we are, indeed, forgiven and it reunites us to the community. A good way for us to begin this process is to pause daily in our busy lives and review the events of each day. How have we hit and how have we missed our mark? Recognizing how we have hit or missed the mark puts us on the journey to salvation. We can then allow the Spirit to well up within us; this develops our hearts to be sorry for the selfish and unilateral choices we have made.

[17] We have called this sense of sorrow by a name: "contrition." Once we have reached this point of awareness and sorrow, it is time for us to reconcile. As in all things, we humans need some visible, tangible, or audible sign to help us see, touch, and hear God's love.

[18] In this matter, the Church has long called us to confess our sins with a priest in a private moment, normally in a reconciliation room within a church building. This conversation, however, can occur anywhere at any time and under any circumstances. We give a name to this conversation with the priest and that name is "confession."

[19] It is probably rare for most people, but there are some ways of sinning that wound us mortally because they are so entirely selfish, so entirely unilateral. They wound us so deeply that we call them "mortal sins." They cross a certain line of reasonableness into the

territory of deep darkness, even if they are done in secret. We know that for us to be truly healed, to be truly reconciled to the gospel, to be truly reunited to the community, and to be truly aware of God's forgiveness, we must discuss these incidents in the sacrament of reconciliation.

[20] But even more minor incidents (called "venial sins") can and should be discussed if we wish to be faithful. Confession is required when mortal sins are committed, and it is encouraged even in cases of venial sin.

Group or personal process

- What are some of the mortal sins we can commit?

- What distinguishes mortal sin from venial sin?

- Why is confession of serious sins so important for our journey of faith?

PART THREE **+ ARTICLES 1458–1484 OF THE *CATECHISM***

Making amends

[21] If we have injured our neighbor by gossip, stealing, or failing to love, we must make that up in order to be truly healed. We give a name to that process of making up. We call it "penance." In the sacrament, the priest assigns us a form of penance in order to help make real what we are doing and deepen our spiritual journey.

[22] We always celebrate this sacrament with a priest, who stands

in the place of Christ for us, offering the same love and the same forgiveness that Christ himself offers. Hence, it is not the priest who forgives us, but Christ. All that the priest hears when we discuss our tendencies to sin remains forever a secret and may never be shared, without exception. We refer to this permanent and confidential state as the "seal of confession" because what we share is sealed forever.

Being reconciled

[23] There is mystery in this, but we know that God never leaves us, no matter how seriously we sin and miss the mark. And yet we do need a sign of this forgiveness and reconciliation. Our human heart is healed and is at peace and has a sense of well-being only after we reconcile. We have a strong sense of being restored or being blessed by this sacrament. God indulges us by offering forgiveness and taking away any punishment resulting from our sins.

WE BELIEVE

This sacrament reconciles us with Christ, the Church, and one another. It increases our spiritual strength to choose what is good and avoid evil.

---

[24] Furthermore, we have the experience of being rejoined to one another as Church, of restoring our bonds of love. We set ourselves on a pattern of life, avoiding the ways we act selfishly and choosing to live more and more in love.

The liturgy of reconciliation

[25] Normally, when we go to celebrate this liturgy, we begin with a blessing, followed by reading the word of God. Then, in a conversational style we discuss with the priest the ways we have sinned and

what the results of that have been. The priest asks us to make up for this by way of a penance, pronounces the words of absolution, offers a prayer of thanksgiving, and gives us a blessing.

[26] This sacrament can also take place within a communal setting. In these celebrations we prepare together, pray in common, and receive a common blessing. The confession of sins occurs after a liturgy of the word. The communal setting emphasizes our joined lives and how we travel on our journeys of faith together.

Group or personal process

- Why is it important for Christians to regularly pause and be reconciled like this? What happens when we don't do this?

- How do you reconcile and make up with your closest friends and family?

- What has been your experience with this sacrament over the years since your first confession?

Prayer

Have mercy on me, O God, according to your steadfast love; according to your abundant mercy blot out my transgressions. Wash me thoroughly from my iniquity, and cleanse me from my sin. For I know my transgressions, and my sin is ever before me. Create in me a clean heart, O God, and put a new and right spirit within me. (Psalm 51:1–3, 10) In your wisdom lead us to confess our sins humbly and honestly and receive your free and generous forgiveness. We pray through Christ, our Lord. Amen.

Session Five

BASED ON ARTICLES 1499–1525 OF THE *CATECHISM OF THE CATHOLIC CHURCH*. TO READ A SUMMARY OF THIS SECTION, SEE *CATECHISM* ARTICLES 1526–1532

Introduction

The sacrament of anointing of the sick confers a special grace on the Christian experiencing the difficulties inherent in the condition of grave illness or old age. Each time a Christian falls seriously ill, he or she may receive the anointing of the sick, and also when, after he or she has received it, the illness worsens. The celebration of the anointing of the sick consists essentially in the anointing of the fore-head and hands of the sick person (in the Roman tradition) or of other parts of the body (in the Eastern tradition), the anointing being accompanied by the liturgical prayer of the celebrant asking for the special grace of this sacrament. The special grace of the anointing of the sick unites the sick person to the Passion of Christ and gives strength, peace, and courage to help the sick person to endure the sufferings of illness or old age.

Scripture

READER: A reading from the Letter of James.

Are any among you suffering? They should pray. Are any cheerful? They should sing songs of praise. Are any among you sick? They should call for the elders of the Church and have them pray over them, anointing them with oil in the name of the Lord. The prayer of faith will save the sick, and the Lord will raise them up; and anyone who has committed sins will be forgiven.

(JAMES 5:13–15)

READER: The word of the Lord.

ALL: Thanks be to God.

PART ONE + ARTICLES 1499–1507 OF THE *CATECHISM*

Be healed

[1] The sacrament of anointing of the sick commends those who are ill to Christ. It immerses them in God so that the energy of God's love might stir up in them the insight of meaning allowing them to see their illness—and even their impending death—as part of the great story of life and journey of faith.

[2] Human suffering and death are perhaps among life's greatest mysteries. They so clearly establish for us our own limits. We are powerless in the face of them—and we face death a little each time we are sick. Illness can lead us to despair, anguish without relief, and even the rejection of love in favor of self-absorption.

[3] Or it can lead to greater maturity, helping us sort out what is most important and even provoking a search for God and deeper desire to love others and be near them. Our ancient forbearers also did not understand the meaning and mystery of illness. Sometimes they blamed God when they were sick and other times believed that God healed them. They even believed that illness was the result of

sin. And with hope pressing in on them, they believed a time would come when illness would be no more.

[4] In revealing God to us, Jesus Christ dealt with illness and healing throughout his life. His compassion for the sick is legendary, and his ability to heal was a sign that the reign of God is close at hand. But the healing of Jesus Christ had the whole person as its object, shifting the focus of our understanding of illness from punishment for sin to the mercy of God.

WE BELIEVE

This sacrament has the purpose of giving special graces to Christians who experience difficulties during illness or old age.

---

[5] The stories of healing by Jesus which the gospels retell are meant to be signs of God's power and the coming of God's reign. They announce a more radical healing, a deeper healing. The mission of Christ was to reveal God's love, to be in his own self a clear sign of love, and indeed, to be love itself. The healing that he offers us is, on a deeper level, related to that. He established a way of life, a journey of faith, and a path to freedom.

[6] He offers liberation from selfishness, loneliness, and sinful choices. We often call this liberation by a name: "salvation"; and this name means, literally, "healing" or "being made whole" or "being saved." Oh, yes, we are healed and saved by Jesus, and this healing gives us the freedom to love.

[7] The Church continues to have the same concern for the sick that Jesus did. Indeed, the gospels tell how Jesus sent his followers out to teach and heal as he himself had been doing. The Gospel of

Mark tells the story of Jesus sending the twelve disciples on mission. We find this in chapter 6, verses 7–13. And later in Mark, the risen Christ renews this call to be healers. Almost certainly the early community saw in Christ the love of God and the wholeness that is possible only when we live as we are created to live.

Group or personal process

- What is the liberation and healing that Jesus promises?

- In your own life, what is one of the ways you experience that?

- Which of the healing stories of Jesus touches your heart most profoundly? Why?

PART TWO + ARTICLES 1508–1516 OF THE *CATECHISM*

The care of the sick

[8] When we speak of healing for the sick, we do not necessarily mean recovery from illness. Grace is God's self-communication to us; it is God giving us God's own self in love. God energizes us for love. Light shines in darkness. Life is stronger than death. When we embrace grace and receive it openly, we find that it is all we need. So that even when we are powerless over illness—cancer, depression, alcoholism, disease, or emotional pain—we are strong.

[9] The Church in its ministry to the sick cares for their needs by operating hospitals, by providing pastoral care, and by guiding them to find meaning in life. Through various means of outreach and support, the Church also cares for the families and friends of those who

are ill and dying. In the early Church there was a tradition of prayer over the sick which has come down to us as a sacrament today.

WE BELIEVE

Each time a Christian falls ill, he or she may receive anointing of the sick. Certainly if one is in danger of death, this sacrament is appropriate.

[10] In the Letter of James, which gives important guidance on how to live our faith on a daily basis, the writer counsels us Christians to put faith into practice, to care for the needy, to have a heart for the materially poor, and to really live what we believe. The writer of this letter urges us to look deeply into the heart of Christ and into our own hearts.

[11] The writer suggests we may sometimes be at war within ourselves, wanting one thing but doing another. This writer urges us to act now! "You do not even know what tomorrow will bring," he reminds us, so get busy! The Letter of James counsels us to be patient like a farmer waiting for seed to sprout. "Strengthen your hearts," we are told.

[12] And this wise writer finally suggests that if any are sick, the elders should pray over them, anointing them with oil. We should confess our sins, come clean, take the first step, admit we are powerless, and, hence, be healed. And this is the basis of our sacrament: we are in the business of helping one another heal.

The sacrament

[13] As we have just seen, there is a long tradition in the Church of anointing when people are sick. But over the centuries, it more and more came to be used only at the point of death. In fact, it even ac-

quired the name "extreme unction," which means "final anointing."

[14] The *Constitution on the Liturgy* at Vatican II asked the Church to revisit this sacrament and to rename it. In article 73 the Constitution suggests the name "anointing of the sick" and reminds us that it is not intended only for those at death's door. In 1972, Pope Paul VI published more guidelines for this sacrament; among other things, he wrote that one who is sick should be anointed with sacred oil on the forehead and hands.

[15] In the Eastern rites, other parts of the body are also anointed. One can receive this sacrament more than once, even within a single illness or as we become frail with old age. Only bishops and priests can anoint, but the context, as much as possible, should be communal.

Group or personal process

- What has been your personal experience with this sacrament? Have you received it or witnessed others receiving it?

- From what sort of situations, memories, conditions, or illnesses have you needed to be healed?

PART THREE + ARTICLES 1517–1525 OF THE *CATECHISM*

How we celebrate

[16] As we have just suggested, this sacrament is liturgical and communal. It is not a private sacrament to be done in secret. It may take place in a family home, a hospital or hospice room, or a church. It

may involve a single person or many people at once. It can be celebrated within the Eucharist and may be preceded by reconciliation.

[17] In any case, the final sacrament of life, of course, should be Eucharist—called "viaticum" when received by the dying, a name that means "food for the journey."

[18] We begin the celebration with God's word as we always do in sacraments, to awaken the faith of the sick person. Then the priest—in silence—lays his hands on them, praying on behalf of the Church before anointing them with sacred oil.

The fruits of this sacrament

[19] All the sacraments, we teach, "give grace." When we say that, we mean that God fills us with divine power. This being filled up with God is real. It is God giving us God's own self. Powerful, indeed. In this sacrament the first gifts of grace are strength, peace, and courage.

WE BELIEVE

The grace of this sacrament unites the sick or dying person to Christ and the community; it strengthens us inwardly to bear our illness with grace; it restores us to health if that is conducive to saving our souls; and it prepares us for death.

---

[20] We are reminded that we live in God, and God's love never ceases no matter how sick or old we are. The Spirit is aroused within us in this sacrament. In a sense this sacrament joins us mysteriously to the dying and rising of Christ, that is, to the paschal mystery. In baptism we entered into the death of the Lord, taking up our own

crosses, putting on Christ like a garment, and following Christ on the journey of faith.

[21] Here we confront that Christian vocation again: embracing our suffering without ever giving up our love, just as Christ did on the cross. This sacrament also joins us to the community. And finally, this sacrament prepares us for the "final journey." It is our final anointing just as baptism was our first anointing.

[22] It brings us full circle on the journey of faith, bringing us peace and the sure knowledge that our home—our true home—is in God; it is also in the community of the Church. By helping us avoid despair, anger, and fear when we are sick, it helps us move forward in peace.

The final step

[23] And, as we have said above, we are also invited to share one last time in the banquet of eternal life that we celebrate while we are living: Eucharist. We are thus initiated ever more deeply into the heart of the Lord by our communion, and we are healed and made ready for death by our anointing.

Group or personal process

- Share a story of someone you know who has died and how their final days of life were a preparation for their journey of faith.

- Why do you think healing the sick was such a major part of the ministry of Jesus? How does it fit into the rest of his mission? And how does it fit into the work of the Church today?

Prayer

Jesus, we come to you as healer and teacher. We call you Lord. In you we find our peace, for you walk beside us in good times and in difficult ones. Grant us the consolation of knowing we will live with you forever if we remain in your love. Give us the courage to face illness and death with the assurance that you are with us, now and forever. Amen.

Session Six

BASED ON ARTICLES 1533–1589 OF THE *CATECHISM OF THE CATHOLIC CHURCH*. TO READ A SUMMARY OF THIS SECTION, SEE *CATECHISM* ARTICLES 1590–1600

Introduction

We conclude our study of the sacraments with a treatment of two sacraments of service: holy orders and matrimony. We begin with holy orders. The whole Church is a priestly people. Through baptism all the faithful share in the priesthood of Christ. This participation is called the "common priesthood of the faithful." The ministerial priesthood differs in essence from the common priesthood of the faithful because it confers a sacred power for the service of the faithful. The ordained ministers exercise their service for the People of God by teaching, divine worship, and pastoral governance. Since the beginning, the ordained ministry has been conferred and exercised in three degrees: that of bishops, that of presbyters, and that of deacons. The sacrament of holy orders is conferred by the laying on of hands followed by a solemn prayer of consecration asking God to grant the ordained the graces of the Holy Spirit required for his ministry.

Scripture

READER: A reading from the Second Letter of Paul to Timothy.

I am reminded of your sincere faith, a faith that lived first in your grandmother Lois and your mother Eunice and now, I am sure, lives in you. For this reason I remind you to rekindle the gift of God that is within you through the laying on of my hands; for God did not give us a spirit of cowardice, but rather a spirit of power and of love and of self-discipline. (2 TIMOTHY 1: 5–7)

READER: The word of the Lord.

ALL: Thanks be to God.

PART ONE ✢ ARTICLES 1533–1547 OF THE *CATECHISM*
We are made for service

[1] Baptism, confirmation, and Eucharist are sacraments of initiation. Anointing and reconciliation are sacraments of healing. Holy orders and matrimony, however, gather these others and go one step further by consecrating or making holy those called to them for service.

[2] Holy orders is a gift of the Spirit to the Church, continuing the mission of Christ in unique and important roles. There are three levels of these roles, and each is designated by receiving holy orders: bishop, priest, deacon. In the ancient world an "order" was a designated group or a governing counsel.

[3] One who joined such a group was said to be "incorporated into an order." Today we speak of "religious orders of women" or "religious orders of men" in the Church. We also speak of the "order of bishop" or the "order of priesthood or deaconate."

[4] Incorporation into the order of bishop, priest, or deacon is ac-

complished by a special rite called, of course, "ordination." This is a liturgical and sacramental action, a public action in the Church which confers the gift of the Holy Spirit on the one being ordained. This gift is one of love and service. The power or energy of love is a sacred power. The visible sign of this sacrament is the laying on of hands by a bishop.

From ancient times

[5] The people of God has always been "a kingdom of priests and a holy nation." But from ancient times the tribe of Levi was set apart for liturgical leadership. Priests of that tribe, called Levites, were consecrated to preside at rites of thanksgiving and reconciliation. We see in this ancient practice the roots of today's ordination.

WE BELIEVE

The ordained ministers exercise their ministry as a service to the People of God by teaching, divine worship, and pastoral governance.

---

[6] Jesus was not from the tribe of Levi, but he established a new priesthood through his own ministry of healing, teaching, prayer, and most of all the paschal mystery: his dying and rising. Christ is the first priest and the only true priest. All others—bishops, priests, deacons, and the faithful people of God—are ministers of Christ.

[7] The whole community of believers—all the baptized—is priestly. We are all called to live a vocation of service: visiting the sick, having a heart for the materially poor, freeing those held captive, and announcing the reign of God. We refer to this as the "common priesthood" of all the faithful, but we distinguish it from what we call the "ministerial priesthood."

[8] Each of these has a certain role in the Church, and this is important. The common priesthood has the role of animating the world with the Spirit of Christ, radically living the gospel, and cultivating deep faith, great hope, and endless charity. This common priesthood flows from baptism and confirmation.

[9] The ministerial priesthood is at the service of the common priesthood. This ministerial priesthood flows from holy orders. Hence we all participate in the saving of the world.

Group or personal process

- How do you see the one priesthood of Christ, in both its expressions (the common and the hierarchical priesthoods), doing the work of the reign of God in your parish community?

- In your own words, how does the role of the ordained differ from that of the baptized in the everyday life of a typical parish?

- What is your role in the common priesthood (if you are not ordained)?

PART TWO + ARTICLES 1548–1571 OF THE CATECHISM

Ordination

[10] Whenever an ordained priest exercises his ministry of service in the Church, he stands in the place of Christ. It is Christ who serves and Christ who acts. This does not imply that priests are per-

fect! We are all subject to that inclination to sin, to be selfish, and to dominate others.

[11] Ordination doesn't make a bishop or priest perfect, but it gives the community a leader through whom Christ's work can be done. It is primarily a ministry of service, just as Christ served us all. This service is carried out through leadership, by bringing "holy order" into church life, by representing Christ sacramentally, and by acting in the name of us all, especially at the Eucharist.

[12] By this we don't mean that a priest is our "delegate" to God. We are all called to pray, to serve, and to love. It is the whole Church that offers the Eucharist.

Three degrees

[13] We speak about ordination in degrees or levels of service. Two of these are ministerial participation in the priesthood of Christ: bishop and priest. The third, deaconate, is intended to help and serve bishops and priests. All three are designated by ordination.

Bishops

[14] The apostles of Christ received the Holy Spirit and took on the leadership of the early Church as a result. Down through the centuries in an unbroken line of succession, bishops have been chosen to continue this ministry. We refer to bishops as having received "the fullness of...holy orders." By this, we designate them as authentic teachers, pastors, and vicars of Christ.

[15] One is made a bishop only when named by the pope and ordained by several other bishops. Each bishop is then entrusted with the pastoral care of a particular local church but shares collegial authority with all other bishops in unity with the pope.

Priests

[16] The bishops, of course, cannot do all the work that lies before the Church in today's world. Therefore, priests are chosen and ordained as coworkers in order that the mission of Christ can be accomplished. Priests are joined with bishops in building up the body of Christ and in sanctifying and ruling the Church.

[17] Hence, priests are ordained and signed with a special grace. The *Dogmatic Constitution on the Church* from Vatican II reminds us in article 28 that priests are to preach the gospel, to shepherd the faithful, and to preside at public worship, especially Eucharist. They do not act on their own, however, because they depend on bishops for their authority; with their bishops, priests of a given diocese form a single priesthood. In their parishes, priests represent the bishop by taking on themselves his duties and having promised him obedience.

Permanent deacons

[18] When a priest is ordained, the bishop and all other priests who are present lay hands on him as a sign of their sharing in this one priesthood. When a permanent deacon is ordained, however, only the bishop lays hands on him as a sign of the permanent deacon's role in service of the bishop. Permanent deacons do not receive ministerial priesthood, but they are given important functions in the parish or diocesan community.

[19] Among other tasks, permanent deacons assist bishops and priests in the celebration of the liturgy, in blessing marriages, in proclaiming the gospel and preaching, in presiding over funerals, and in dedicating themselves to the various ministries of charity.

Group or personal process

- How do you experience the "servant leadership" of your own local bishop, priests, and permanent deacons?

- How does their ministry support your own?

How we ordain

[20] When bishops, priests, or deacons are ordained in the Church, as many of the faithful as possible should be present. Ordination to each of these three degrees is similar and normally takes place within the Eucharist. The essential moment of ordination is the laying on of hands and the prayer of consecration. There are other rites that surround this essential moment and that symbolically express the mystery of God's grace among us in the priesthood: the presentation of the one to be ordained, an instruction by the bishop, and the litany of the saints.

[21] Bishops and priests are both anointed with sacred chrism. Bishops are presented with the gospels, a ring, a miter, and a crosier that signify their role as shepherds. Priests are handed the offertory gifts of bread, wine, money, and other offerings and urged to bring holy order to them. Deacons are presented with the Book of the Gospels and urged to proclaim it well.

[22] We believe it is Christ himself who ordains through the actions of our bishops. Hence, only validly ordained bishops can ordain other bishops, priests, or deacons.

[23] In the Catholic Church only baptized males can be ordained. Only those men who have been found suitable are invited to receive this sacrament. In the Latin tradition, all ordained ministers except permanent deacons must be men of faith who live a celibate life and who intend to remain celibate forever in order to serve more fully.

[24] In the Eastern rites, married men can be ordained as priests and deacons, a longstanding practice. In both the Eastern and the Latin rite, unmarried men who have been ordained can no longer marry.

WE BELIEVE

Holy orders is conferred by the laying on of hands followed by a solemn prayer of consecration. The ordaining ministers ask God to give the ordained the grace of the Holy Spirit for his ministry. Only men can be ordained.

---

[25] The sacrament of holy orders, like the sacraments of baptism and confirmation, permanently changes a person, creating a way-of-being that never ends. For this reason ordination cannot be repeated and no one is temporarily ordained. Even if a priest, bishop, or deacon ceases work or for some reason is discharged, they remain ordained.

[26] Like all sacraments, ordination gives grace. For the bishop, it is the grace of strength to guide his Church, to proclaim the gospel without fear, and to be a model for the faithful. For the priest, it is the grace of fidelity to announce the Good News, to believe what is preached, and to live what is believed. For the deacon, it is the grace of service to obey the bishop, to serve with humility, and to work with charity.

Group or personal process

- What does it mean to you that the Church places so much emphasis on "service" as the form of leadership and governance in order to most fully reflect the way of Christ?

- Think over the life of your own parish community. Who is not being served well at the present time? Who is not welcomed? And on the other hand, in what areas does your parish serve people well?

Prayer

You call us all to service, O God, and you empower us through your Holy Spirit to be your hands and feet in today's Church. May those of us called to ordination be men of dedication, faith, prayer, and humility. May your wisdom be their guide and your presence in their lives lead them to holiness. Thank you for sending the Spirit to us through the sacrament of holy orders. We pray in Jesus' name. Amen.

Session Seven

MATRIMONY

BASED ON ARTICLES 1601–1658 OF THE *CATECHISM OF THE CATHOLIC CHURCH*. TO READ A SUMMARY OF THIS SECTION, SEE *CATECHISM* IN ARTICLES 1659–1666

Introduction

We close our study of the sacraments by considering the wonderful and life-changing moment when two people get married—matrimony. The marriage covenant, by which a man and a woman form with each other an intimate communion of life and love, has been founded and endowed with its own special laws by the Creator. By its very nature, it is ordered to the good of the couple as well as to the generation and education of children. Marriage is based on the consent of the contracting parties, that is, on their will to give themselves, each to the other, mutually and definitively, in order to live a covenant of faithful and fruitful love. Unity, permanence, and openness to fertility (for those of a childbearing age) are essential to marriage. The Christian home is the place where children receive their first proclamation of the faith. For this reason, the family home is rightly called "the domestic church," a community of grace and prayer, and a school of human virtues and of Christian charity.

Scripture

READER: A reading from the Gospel of Matthew.

Some Pharisees came to him, and to test him they asked, "Is it lawful for a man to divorce his wife for any cause?" He answered, "Have you not read that the one who made them at the beginning 'made them male and female,' and said, 'For this reason a man shall leave his father and mother and be joined to his wife, and the two shall become one flesh'? So they are no longer two, but one flesh. Therefore what God has joined together, let no one separate." (MATTHEW 19:3-6)

READER: The word of the Lord.

ALL: Thanks be to God.

PART ONE + ARTICLES 1601–1615 OF THE *CATECHISM*

Love!

[1] For us Catholics, the partnership between a man and a woman in a lifelong marriage covenant with each other, where they look after each other's needs and raise children together as they are able, is a sacrament. It is a holy covenant and it reflects God. From beginning to end, sacred Scripture speaks of this mystery of love.

[2] It is within our very nature, our being, to love and commit ourselves in love like this. Because it is so deeply imbedded in our nature, we believe God is the author of marriage. Marriage is rooted in a loving relationship of mutuality. We are, after all, created in the image of the Triune God. It is very good in the Creator's eyes.

[3] Such mutual love, then, becomes fruitful: guarding creation, caring for it, and loving it. When possible, children result from sexual love and this fulfills our divine vocation. Sometimes, of course, marriage is not about love: Couples fight. One dominates the other. They can

be jealous. One or the other may have sex outside of their marriage. They can grow to hate each other and live with deep discord. They sometimes separate and no longer live together, or they even divorce.

[4] All this selfish and unilateral behavior results from that inner tendency we all have to "miss the mark" and live sinfully. This has been true from the very beginning of time, from the first relationships between humans. And what is the answer? How do we overcome this selfishness? Only through grace. Grace is the reception into our lives of God's life offered through Christ and realized through the Spirit who lives in our hearts.

WE BELIEVE

The purposes of marriage are to support the mutual love of the couple and the bearing and education of children. We believe that Christ raised marriage to the dignity of a sacrament.

---

[5] If the love we share has this divine source, it is mutual and respectful and it helps the couple shape a right relationship. It gives us the ability and power to forgive, to be generous to each other, to reconcile over and over again, to remain faithful sexually, and to live as true partners in love.

[6] Down through the centuries we have come to realize more and more clearly what we believe flows from God. Gradually we have come to believe that women should be protected from arbitrary divorce and that they should not be dominated by men, according to article 1610 of the *Catechism*.

[7] Jesus teaches quite clearly that marriage is permanent. We find this teaching in the Gospel of Matthew, chapter 19. Jesus has been

asked by some Pharisees about whether is it lawful for a man to divorce his wife for any cause. "They are no longer two, but one flesh," he tells them. "Therefore what God has joined together, let no one separate."

[8] The Church attaches great importance to this and also to Jesus' own presence at wedding feasts like the one in Cana. In his teachings and practice, Jesus was saying that we *can* live in love. He revealed the power of that love: if we die to ourselves in love of another, if we "take up our cross daily," in the words of the gospel, and give ourselves in love, *we can do this*. This is the grace of marriage: to give ourselves in love.

Group or personal process

- How do you experience the grace of love in your own life, whether or not you are married? How do you experience "taking up your cross daily" as you love others?

- How does marriage support the Christian community?

PART TWO + **ARTICLES 1616–1631 OF THE** *CATECHISM*
Christ loves the Church

[9] The Scriptures use a mysterious simile to describe how we as the People of God are related to Christ. Christ loves the Church, St. Paul tells us, as husbands and wives love one another. Christian marriage becomes a sign for us of that wonderful spousal love that Christ has for us.

[10] We must also take pains to mention, of course, that not everyone is called to marriage. We must see married life as a vocation, an inner calling whose source is God. There is another vocation, of equal dignity, and also realized as an inner calling: virginity for the sake of the kingdom of God. Both of these states are an unfolding of baptismal grace and both are rooted in love. Indeed, Christ himself seems to have been called to the latter state in life.

Celebrating the sacrament

[11] When Catholics marry it is usually celebrated at Mass in the Latin tradition. This connects the commitment of the couple with the covenant of Christ and the Church. By receiving communion as part of the ceremony, the couple symbolically forms "one body in Christ." Couples can best prepare for this by first celebrating sacramental reconciliation, opening their hearts to lives of love, and committing themselves to do everything possible to avoid selfishness.

WE BELIEVE

Marriage is based on the covenant of the two parties, on their will to give themselves to each other and on their freedom to give full consent to the marriage bond.

---

[12] In the Latin tradition, the spouses themselves are the ministers of the sacrament, with the priest or deacon and the community as witnesses. In the Eastern tradition, the minister is the priest, who receives the consent of the couple and then crowns them as a sign of their covenant. All liturgies of marriage are filled with blessings and moments of prayer during which we call on the Spirit to live in the couple's hearts.

[13] In order for a couple to marry, they must be free to do so: freely giving their consent under no constraints to do so and having no impediments of law. If there is no consent, there is no marriage. They must express their consent in the company of witnesses as a free act of their own will with no external coercion or fear. The freedom to give consent must also be present. If such consent was not freely given, if such an act of will was not expressed, or if an impediment, even unseen, was present, the marriage may be declared void. We refer to such declarations as "annulments."

[14] The couple normally states their intentions to a priest or deacon who acts as witness on behalf of the community in the context of a marriage liturgy. Marriage is a state of life in the Church complete with rights and duties; such public weddings help couples understand this and remain faithful.

[15] We may even speak of it as "the order of marriage," which is why celebrating it in a liturgical setting is so important. For this reason preparation for marriage is also very important, especially in our age when so many marriages end in divorce.

[16] Marriage is a sacred, holy covenant, entered into by the couple in the presence of a priest or deacon with selected witnesses in the presence of the whole community, but it is authored by God.

[17] Special permission to marry is needed for couples who are not both Catholic, whether one is another Christian or a non-Christian. In all these cases, care should be taken that such marriages do not lead to tension within the home, especially regarding the children. Couples in such situations can grow spiritually and each gain from the other's faith.

Group or personal process

- Why do you think the Church sees marriage as a "vocation"?

- What special challenges does marriage face in today's world? How can we help couples work through difficulties and avoid divorce?

PART THREE ✛ **ARTICLES 1632–1658 OF THE** *CATECHISM*

The bond

[18] When a couple marries, freely giving their consent to one another, the commitment is sealed by God. Indeed, the *Pastoral Constitution on the Church in the Modern World* from Vatican II made this clear in article 48, where it says that "authentic married love is caught up in divine love." We speak of the relationship between husband and wife as a "bond," meaning a "sealed commitment."

[19] This marriage bond has been established by God, who is the author of love. Because of this, we believe that once a marriage is declared publicly and consummated through sexual love, it can never be dissolved. Not even the Church has the power to break such a bond.

The grace

[20] The grace of marriage helps the couple strengthen their bond, receive children lovingly, and care for one another. Christ is the source of this grace. Christ dwells within the marriage, helping them love one another with supernatural, tender, and fruitful love.

Sexual love

[21] Sexual love involves the total person: physical attraction, deep instincts to continue the human family, great affection for one another, and a profound sense of unity and oneness. It is really much more than a physical act because the whole person is involved and because the couple is open to conceiving a child.

[22] For us Catholics, sex is one of the "outward signs" the sacrament of matrimony. It is holy and blessed. By its very nature, therefore, sexual loving requires spouses to be faithful. They are making a profound gift to one another and taking a profound risk at the same time. For this reason, having more than one spouse, or more than one sexual partner, or a sexual partner without marriage, is not within the Christian practice.

WE BELIEVE

The Christian home is a domestic church; it is where children hear about the faith for the first time. Homes are communities of grace and prayer, and they are schools of human virtue and Christian charity.

---

[23] A follower of Christ comes to see sexual activity as an expression of something much greater. It is not temporary or arbitrary or casual. It can seem difficult or even impossible to bind oneself for life to another human being. But such bonding is a reflection of God, as we have said above, and it is the Good News of Christ. God binds the divine heart to us humans in the very same way: permanently, unconditionally, and freely.

[24] And yet there are some situations in which living together is no longer possible: the bond has broken down, or there is violence in the home, or there is infidelity. The Church teaches that such a

couple is still married and is not free to marry again even if civilly divorced. Only if a couple can show that they had an impediment to their marriage or that their marriage consent was defective can it be declared void—which frees them to marry again.

[25] The Church has a deep pastoral commitment to people in these situations. They are not separated from the Church, but they are limited in how they may participate. They remain baptized and called to lives of holiness: to listen to the word of God, to attend Mass, to pray often, to perform works of charity and justice, to bring up their children in the faith, and to live in grace just as all Christians are called.

Children
[26] It is the purpose of marriage that the couple lives in mutual love and receives children generously as much as they are able. Parents hand on to their children the love which they themselves share. They provide a foundation for the children's faith, educate them about life, and help them develop in every way. Couples who do not have children may still have a wonderful bond and lives full of meaning and purpose. Their marriage can radiate the fruitfulness of charity, hospitality, and sacrifice.

Households of faith
[27] We live in households of faith, whether we live alone or with others, and whether we are married, single, or in religious life. Christ himself lived in such a household, and the early Church gathered in that forum as well. In our own day and age, this can be a real challenge, which is why we now speak of households as "domestic churches."

[28] Indeed, *we are the Church* living our everyday lives at home and work, at school and play. Our homes are where the Church

lives. The household of faith is where we live our baptismal priesthood: serving each other, caring for the materially poor, watching out for neighbors, and living with charity for all. Here is where we practice forgiveness and learn to offer it beyond the home. Here is where we experience the joy of love, of shared tasks, and even of shared prayer.

[29] Here, in short, is where we live "community life," which is a life reflecting the love of the Trinity. This is also true even for those who live alone for whatever reason: as widows or widowers, as single people, as persons having been abandoned, or persons in poverty or in refugee status, or persons who are forced to this situation because of violence or war, or persons who choose to live alone out of a sense of mission to others. The doors of all our homes should also be open to them, and we should pay special attention to their needs for community life.

Group or personal process

- How do you make your home into a "household of faith"?

- Read faith statements #24–25 again. How can we support and love people who are going through the pain and difficulty of broken relationships?

- What is your vocation in life? How do you hear God calling you?

Prayer

O God, you are the author of marriage, bringing us together in mutual love and charity. Send your Spirit among us to help us reduce the power of darkness that leads to selfish and sinful behaviors. May your Spirit fill us with the fire of your divine love, shared in the Blessed Trinity. Give us hearts that are ready to serve those with whom we share daily life in our homes. May charity and love prevail each day of our life. We make this prayer through Christ, our Lord, now and forever. Amen.